At the Movie Theater

Mary Sue O'Bannon
Illustrated by Larry O'Bannon

Photography approved in advance by staff of Goodrich Quality Theaters Capital 8 in Jefferson City, Missouri, and used with permission.

AKA-Publishing
AKA:ʏoʟᴙ

Published by
AKA-Publishing
Columbia Missouri

ISBN: 978-1-942168-20-1

This book is dedicated to my grandson, Joey, who posed for pictures, his parents, Shelly and Greg, and to his brother, Matt, who is my writing consultant.

Thank you to the staff and parents at Easter Seals Disability Services in Columbia, Missouri for feedback and to Goodrich Capital 8 Theaters in Jefferson City, Missouri for allowing photos.

At home I watch movies on the couch with my mom and dad. My mom always makes popcorn.

Today I am going to the movie theater with my mom and dad. I wait in line while my dad buys the tickets.

Then I stand in line at the concession stand. I smell popcorn.

After we get popcorn and drinks, I wait in line to give my ticket to the usher.

I walk down the hall to the room where our movie is showing. It is very dark inside. The movie screen is huge.

Our movie does not start right away. There are previews of movies that are coming soon. Some of the previews are scary. I close my eyes during the scary part.

Finally our movie starts. My mom says I have to be quiet so that everyone can hear the movie.

I eat some popcorn. It gets my hands greasy. My mom gives me a napkin to wipe my hands. I take a drink of my soda and put it in the cup holder.

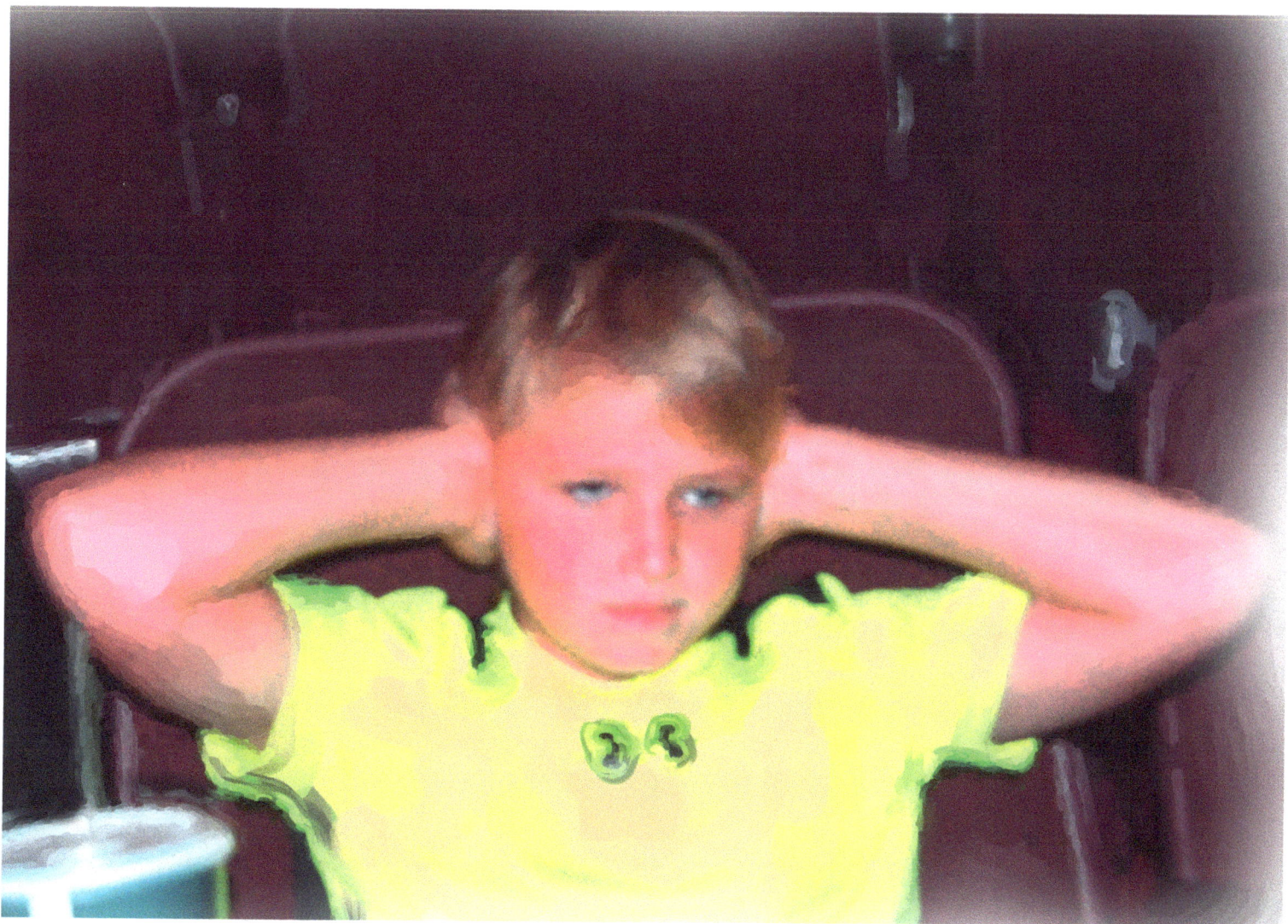

There is a funny part of the movie. All of the people in the theater laugh. It is very loud. I cover my ears until the laughing stops.

When the movie is over, the lights come on. It is very bright after being in the dark theater.

When we get in the car, my dad asks me if I liked going to the theater. I think about it. It wasn't as scary as I thought it would be and the movie was good. Dad says that we can see another movie next week.

Parent tips:

Use the blank lines below each tip to add your own observations and tips.

• Read this book several times before going to the movie theater.

_____

_____

• The earliest matinée will be less crowded than later shows. Avoid opening weekend.

_____

_____

• Prepare the child for what is coming next. Tell them when the lights will go off at the beginning of the movie and when they will come on at the end.

_____

_____

• Choose the movie carefully. A good choice is a sequel to a movie that the child has watched and liked. Another good choice is an area of interest.

_____

_____

• Watch the online movie trailer with your child.

_____

_____

• Let the child tell or show you what bothers him or her and follow the child's lead.

_____

_____

• Give your child calming techniques that they specifically use. Let them hold a quiet toy or preferred object. Give deep pressure if that is calming to them.

_____

_____

• If your child doesn't like or can't eat movie theater food, bring a favorite snack. You might want to call the manager, explain the need and make sure that this is allowed.

_____

_____

• If your child cannot handle the regular movie theater environment, some theaters have movies for children with sensory needs. These movies have increased lighting and reduced sound. Children can move around.

_____

_____

www.ingramcontent.com/pod-product-compliance
Lightning Source LLC
Chambersburg PA
CBHW041637040426

42448CB00024B/3501